A snake's day

T0372093

On a hot day,
snakes come out
to rest in the sun.
The bright patterns
will amaze you!

3

Snakes like to stay in the sunlight for a big part of the day.

5

This snake slithers its
way across the sand.
It makes zigzag tracks.

Escape now, frog! Do not
delay! You cannot play
games with a snake.

A lizard makes a good snack for a snake. The snake can gulp down the lizard as if it was a steak.

When a snake has a big,
big lunch, it may be full
for days and days.

Some snakes lay eggs.
They lay their eggs in a
safe spot. They may lay
them in soil, mud or sand.

Some snakes stay with their eggs. Some lay their eggs and go away. Little snakes slither off into the daylight.

A snake makes its way up a great tree. Slither, slither. It will stay hot in the sun.

The day is ending.
The snake makes its way
back down the tree.

Snakes need safe spots to stay for the night. This snake sleeps in a cave.

Words to blend

day	snakes	amaze
stay	way	makes
away	escape	delay
play	games	steak
may	lay	safe
daylight	great	cave

Before reading

Synopsis: This book explores some of the many things that snakes get up to during the day.

Review phonemes and graphemes: /f/ ph; /w/ wh

Focus phoneme: /ai/   **Focus graphemes:** ay, a-e, ea

Book discussion: Look at the cover, and read the title together. Talk about snakes – what do children already know about them? Share their ideas. Ask: *What do you think a snake does in the day? What do you think we might learn about snakes?*

Link to prior learning: Remind children that the sound /ai/ as in 'rain' can also be spelled 'ay', 'a-e' and 'ea'. Turn to pages 8–9 and ask children to find a word with each spelling of the /ai/ sound (makes, snake, steak, may, days).

Vocabulary check: delay: be late or slow – 'do not delay!' means 'do not be slow!'

Decoding practice: Display the words 'amaze', 'delay', 'great' and 'snake'. Can children circle the letter string that makes the /ai/ sound, and read each word?

Tricky word practice: Display the word 'little' and ask children to circle the tricky part of this word ('le' which makes the /l/ sound). Practise reading and writing this word.

After reading

Apply learning: Discuss the book. Ask: *What do you think was the most interesting fact about snakes? Have you ever seen a snake in real life?*

Comprehension

• What do snakes like to do when it is hot? (come out to rest in the sun)

• Can snakes climb? (yes)

• Where do snakes go at night? (safe spots like caves)

Fluency

• Pick a page that most of the group read quite easily. Ask them to reread it with pace and expression. Model how to do this if necessary.

• Challenge children to turn to page 7 and read the text as if the frog was in a lot of danger. Encourage them to pay attention to the exclamation marks and read those parts with more expression.

• Practise reading the words on page 17.

Tricky words review

come	out	full
the	their	you
like	of	do
they	go	into
little	was	some